Turbulent Planet

Crumbling Earth
Erosion & Landslides

Mary Colson

Raintree

Chicago, Illinois

For information, address the publisher:
Raintree, 100 N. LaSalle, Suite 1200, Chicago, IL 60602
Printed and bound in China
08 07
10 9 8 7 6 5 4 3 2

Library of Congress Cataloging-in-Publication Data
Colson, Mary,
  Crumbling earth / Mary Colson.
      p. cm. -- (Turbulent planet)
Includes index.
Summary: Discusses some of the forces that change land structures on
earth, focusing on the process of erosion.
  ISBN 1-4109-0586-1 (lib. bdg.), 1-4109-1024-5 (Pbk.)
  ISBN 978-1-4109-0586-4 (lib. bdg.), 978-1-4109-1024-0 (Pbk.)
  1. Geodynamics--Juvenile literature. 2. Erosion--Juvenile literature.
3. Geology, Structural--Juvenile literature. [1. Erosion. 2.
Geodynamics. 3. Geology.] I. Title. II. Series: Colson, Mary,
1961- Turbulent planet.
  QE501.25.G36 2004
  551.3'02--dc21
                                2003008569

Acknowledgments
The publisher would like to thank the following for permission to reproduce photographs.
P. 4 Popperfoto, pp. 4–5, 5 (middle), 14–15 EPA/PA Photos; pp. 5, 39 (bottom) D. Fleetham, Silvestris/FLPA; pp. 5 (top), 26 T. C. Middleton/Oxford Scientific Films; p. 6 Silvestris Fotoservice/FLPA; pp. 6–7 Getty Images Imagebank; p. 7 Roland Mayr/Oxford Scientific Films; p. 9 NASA; pp. 10, 37 Rex Features; pp. 10–11 John Downer/Oxford Scientific Films; p. 11 USDA/FLPA; pp. 12, 16–17, 17, 28--29, 36–37 Corbis; pp. 12–13, 45 Lloyd Cluff/Corbis; p. 13 Bettmann/Corbis; p. 14 David Tipling/Oxford Scientific Films; p. 15 Alastair Shay/Oxford Scientific Films; p. 16 Mark Newman/FLPA; p. 18 Kynan Bazley/OSF; pp. 18–19 Jonathan Blair/Corbis; p. 19 NASA/Science Photo Library; p. 20 Martin Keene/PA Photos; pp. 20–21 Ron Watts/Corbis; p. 21 Alamy/World Wide Picture Library; p. 22 Chris Ison/PA Photos; pp. 23, 30, 43 Associated Press; p. 24 Elio Ciol/Corbis; pp. 24–24 Skyscan; p. 25 James L. Amos/Corbis; pp. 26–27 Magnum; p. 27 Kim Kulish, Saba/Corbis; p. 29 (right) Hasler, Peirce, Palaniappan, Manyin/NASA Goddard Library for Atmospheres; pp. 30–31 Annie Griffiths Belt/Corbis; pp. 32–33 Bob Gomel/Corbis; p. 33 David Butow/Corbis; p. 34 Keren Su/Oxford Scientific Films; pp. 34–35 Richard Packwood/Oxford Scientific Films; p. 35 Andrew Park, SAL/Oxford Scientific Films; p. 36 Wendy Dennis/FLPA; pp. 38–39 Galen Rowell/Corbis; p. 38 Oxford Scientific Films/Stan Osolinski; p. 40 Martha Holmes/Naturpl; pp. 40–41 E. & D. Hosking/FLPA; p. 42 (left) Tony Page/Ecoscene; p. 42 (right) Andy Rockall/Ecoscene.
Cover photograph reproduced with permission of Corbis.

Contents

Some words appear in bold, **like this.** You can find out what they mean by looking in the glossary. You can also look out for them in the "Wild Words" box at the bottom of each page.

Our Crumbling Earth

△ A mudslide covers a car.

Sudden change

All of a sudden, the ground under your feet starts to shake. As you struggle to stay standing, the whole world starts to swing and sway. You cannot keep your balance. Everything is starting to fall down.

You look up to see the hillside starting to move. Moving slowly at first, the loose earth quickly becomes an **avalanche** of mud and rocks. It streams down the hill toward your town. As it falls, it gathers speed and grows in size. It knocks down trees and gathers more earth and huge rocks. The ground has stopped shaking, but the land has started to slide. Nothing can stop it. As earth races downhill, huge rocks tumble and crush animals, crops, and buildings.

avalanche   mass of snow, ice, rocks, or mud falling quickly down a mountain
erosion   wearing away of the earth's surface

Panic

The landslide rushes down, crushing houses and burying cars. It is getting faster and bigger all the time. Roads are blocked and transportation is at a standstill. People are screaming and trying to outrun the moving earth. They try to gather a few **precious** belongings before it is too late. Some escape with nothing but their lives.

Panic sets in as everyone rushes to find their loved ones. Names are shouted. People help each other dig and search. There is no time to waste. With the rain starting to fall, another landslide could happen at any moment.

Find out later...

Is all **erosion** harmful?

How many landslides happen each year around the world?

What different types of people study erosion?

precious   valuable, important

World in Motion

The surface of the earth is changing all the time. Most of the changes are so small you cannot see them. Some changes are very noticeable. **Avalanches,** fires, and landslides are some of the most dramatic examples of sudden change.

Creeping earth

The surface of the earth can change in many different ways. High winds swirl around mountains and through **valleys,** knocking off bits of rock and picking up soil and dust. Sand carried by the wind wears away at rocks. This can create fantastic shapes. Rain batters down on fields and rivers, washing away land. **Glaciers,** or ice rivers, carve mountains into amazing shapes and create valleys. Finally, the actions of the more than six billion human beings who live on the earth affect it every single day.

△ Liquid rock bursts out of volcanoes and hardens, building up domes of new land.

glacier   slow-moving river of ice
process   series of steps

This **process** of change is called **erosion,** and it is happening all the time. Some erosion is natural. Some of it is caused by humans. Some erosion is good and some is very bad. Erosion is what happens when the surface of rock or soil is worn away by wind, water, air, fire, and humans on the planet.

Natural cycle

Many of the changes are normal processes that create some of the planet's most impressive natural wonders. Millions of tourists visit the Grand Canyon in Arizona every year to marvel at the rock patterns, colors, and beautiful scenery. This is one example of how the earth's surface has changed shape over millions of years—and it is still changing today.

Changing earth

- The Grand Canyon has been shaped over nearly one billion years.

- Each year there are thousands of landslides and avalanches. Luckily, most take place high up in mountains and far away from people.

More than five million people visit the Grand Canyon every year. ▽

△ Strong waves batter and shape the rocks along the coastline.

Earth data

- The earth's crust can be from 4 to 56 miles (6.5 to 90 kilometers) thick.

- The mantle is 1,800 miles (2,900 kilometers) thick.

- The core is 2,140 miles (3,450 kilometers) thick.

This cross section of the earth shows the different parts. ▽

In order to understand some of the natural **erosion,** or land change, that is happening, we need to take a look at how the earth is made up.

Three-part planet

Our planet is made up of three main layers. In the very middle is the **core,** a mass of ultrahot metals. Scientists can only **estimate** how hot the core is, but it is thought to be around 9,932 °F (5,500 °C). That is as hot as the Sun's surface. The outer core is liquid and the inner core is solid. Next to the core is the **mantle.** This layer is made up of melted rock. On top of the mantle comes the earth's **crust.** This is an outer layer of rock. All of the water and land that we know sit on top of it.

Jagged jigsaw

The earth's surface, or crust, is not in one piece. It is broken up into about 30 main pieces, or plates. Some of these plates are enormous. For example, the entire continent of Africa sits on one and all of North America is on another.

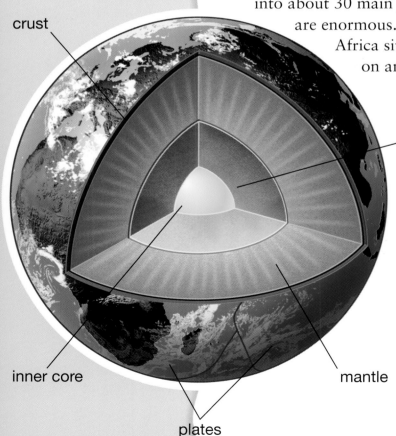

crust

outer core

inner core

mantle

plates

The Earth's Plate Margins

—— **Constructive margin** Two plates move away from each other

▲▲ **Destructive margin** Oceanic crust moves toward continental crust and sinks beneath the continental rock

—— **Collision zone** Plates made of continental crust move toward each other and crumple upward to form fold mountains

▲▼ **Conservative margin** Two plates move past each other

continent   one of the earth's seven large land masses
erode   slowly wear away

Heat escaping from the earth's core causes these massive plates to move and press against each other. This movement creates mountains, **valleys,** seas, and earthquakes. It can even make volcanoes erupt. The plates move against each other at different speeds and in different directions. This movement of the plates is called **plate tectonics,** and it creates and destroys landscapes.

The ground that we stand on is changing all the time. The shapes of the **continents** are changing very slowly as waves **erode** the coasts and earthquakes crumble the land.

The Atlantic Ocean is ▷ getting wider. The Eurasian plate is moving away from the North American plate by about 2 inches (5 centimeters) every year.

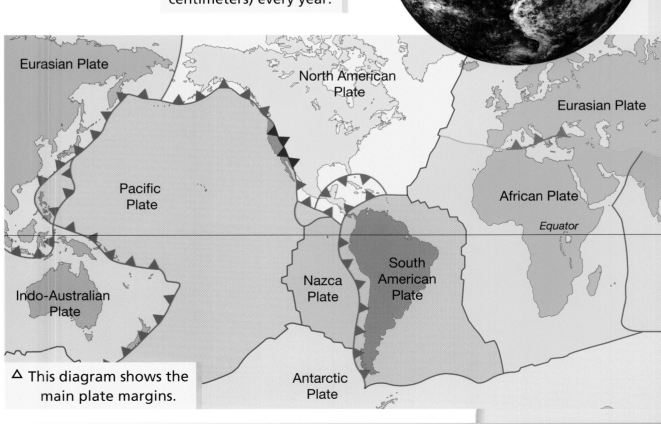

Eurasian Plate

North American Plate

Eurasian Plate

Pacific Plate

African Plate

Equator

Indo-Australian Plate

Nazca Plate

South American Plate

Antarctic Plate

△ This diagram shows the main plate margins.

mantle   extremely hot gases and liquid rock that surround the earth's core
plate tectonics   movement of the earth's plates

Earthquake in India, 2001

After a powerful earthquake, the town of Bhuj lay in heaps of twisted concrete. Buildings were torn in two. It was not safe to live in over 90 percent of Bhuj.

△ There was no electricity, no running water, and no shelter in most of Bhuj after the earthquake.

Plates at war

Something destructive is bound to occur when two massive sheets of rock press against each other or pull apart. Earthquakes happen when two plates grind past each other and stick. The pressure between the two plates builds up so much that one plate has to give way. As it gives way, the ground moves.

When **shockwaves** from an earthquake reach the surface, the top of the earth's **crust** crumbles. Buildings tumble and roads crack. On January 26, 2001, an earthquake struck the town of Bhuj in India. Bhuj was directly above the **focus,** or starting point, of the earthquake. This point on the surface is called the **epicenter.**

eruption   explosion of a volcano
focus   source of an earthquake deep underground

Chain reaction

Sometimes, when plates move deep underground, they set off a chain of events on the surface of the planet. This is called a chain reaction. One way these underground movements are seen on the surface is when a volcano erupts. This can cause a lot of damage and **erosion** of the earth's surface.

Deep underground, extremely hot **molten,** or melted, rock and gas are under great pressure. Slowly, this **magma** melts the rock above it and moves upward. It pushes through holes in the earth's crust, called **vents,** and makes new plate, or crust. As the magma rises up, it causes movement in the earth's crust and can start earthquakes.

Volcanic explosion

One of the largest **eruptions** of the 20th century occured after an earthquake. On May 18, 1980, Mount St. Helens, in Washington, was shaken by a quake. The volcano erupted violently. An **avalanche** of rock and mud moved at 150 mi (240 km) per hour.

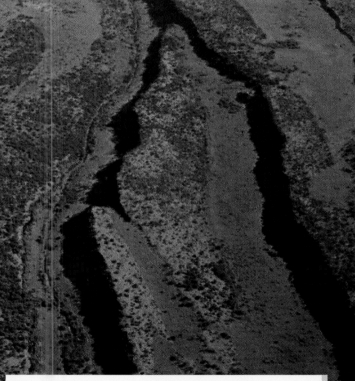

△ The Montanas del Fuego (Fire Mountains) in Lanzarote, an island in Spain, are a group of **extinct** volcanoes that formed at the northwest margin of the African plate.

△ Over 200 sq mi (500 sq km) of forest was destroyed by the Mount St. Helens eruption.

magma   extremely hot molten rock and gas underground
shockwaves   forces that are created by an earthquake deep underground

Fragile Planet

Did you know . . . ?

After the earthquake in 1906, San Francisco burned for three days. The fire did more damage than the original quake.

The earth is more **fragile** than it looks. Here are some ways natural forces shape the surface of our planet.

San Francisco shake

An earthquake is a shaking of the earth's **crust.** Very often, the real destruction happens after the ground has stopped shaking. In 1906 an earthquake shook the city of San Francisco. It took just 48 seconds of shaky ground to cause millions of dollars of damage. Land cracked and split and roads were **buckled.** The shaking broke gas pipes, and the city was quickly in flames. Fire raged through the wooden buildings.

This is the San Andreas Fault ▷ in California. The Pacific Plate and the North American Plate meet here. They have been slowly pushing past each other for years.

buckle   twist or bend out of shape
fragile   delicate

The 1906 quake was the first time an earthquake hit a region that had been studied carefully. Scientists measured everything before and after the earthquake. They learned a lot about how the plates of the earth's crust move against each other. They studied how earthquakes **erode** the surface of the planet.

Terrifying tsunamis

Earthquakes can start landslides, cause flooding, make volcanoes **erupt,** and spark fires. They can also set off big ripples of energy across the surface of the oceans.

These ripples cause huge waves, or **tsunamis.** The waves can be up to 100 feet (30 meters) high, but are usually between 10 and 50 feet (3 and 15 meters). Tsunamis travel across the ocean at an average speed of 470 miles (750 kilometers) per hour. The waves grow even taller as they reach the coastline. The huge rush of water damages rock and washes away soil.

△ About 30 city blocks were damaged or destroyed in Anchorage, Alaska, by a 1964 earthquake.

tsunami   huge ocean wave caused by earthquake, landslide, or volcanic eruption

Some rocks are softer than others, and they erode, or break up, quickly. Limestone is a very tough rock, but it can still be eroded. Rivers, sea, wind, and acid rainwater can all change limestone.

High-level danger

People who live high above sea level in hills or mountains may be safe from floods. But they face danger from another dramatic way that the earth is **eroded**. Landslides occur all over the world and for all sorts of reasons. A landslide happens when rocks and earth slip and tumble down hillsides. Landslides cause **erosion** as they change the face and shape of hillsides. Earthquakes, heavy rains, and human mistakes can all cause landslides.

Quake wrecks El Salvador

In January 2001 a powerful earthquake struck parts of Central America, including the small country of El Salvador. Thousands of buildings were destroyed. Roads were blocked and power was cut off. Many people were killed when the quake caused a landslide. Hundreds of houses were buried when thick mud slid down a mountain.

Over 500,000 people were left homeless by this landslide in Honduras, South America, in 1998. The slide was **triggered** by heavy rain. ▷

△ This rock formation in Ireland is known as the Limestone Pavement.

severe   very bad or serious
species   type of plant or animal

Volcano slides onto village

In November 2001 a landslide from a volcano buried a village in Nicaragua. Matters were made worse by **severe** flooding in the area. Helicopters tried to reach the village, but over 50 people were killed before help arrived. The mudslide was caused by heavy rainfall. The slopes of the volcano simply slid down, forming a mud river. This got faster and faster and gathered more and more earth as it fell. The village did not stand a chance.

Caving in

The largest cave in the world is in the Gunung Mulu National Park in Malaysia. The cave is 0.4 miles (700 meters) long and 230 feet (70 meters) high.

△ Rock erosion can have many good effects. Caves provide homes for hundreds of **species** of plants and animals.

trigger   cause something

Sometimes rocks move quickly and sometimes they move slowly. But over time, the results can be dramatic. As rocks move, they **erode** other rocks and soil and can create new natural wonders in their place.

This multicolored rock formation in Western Australia is known as "The Wave." It is 49 feet (15 meters) high and was shaped by erosion. ▽

Uluru

Some of the oldest rocks on the earth are also the most famous. Uluru, or "Ayer's Rock," in Australia is one of the most recognizable rocks in the world. It was formed over 500 million years ago. Sand piled up on the bottom of an ocean that once covered the middle of Australia. As a result, this huge sandstone rock was created. Over the years, wind and rain have beaten at the rock and eroded the surface of it.

The land around Uluru was once the same height as the rock. Millions of years of erosion left only the rock standing. ▽

Fragile facts

- The base of Uluru is 5 miles (8 km) around.

- Uluru is over 980 feet (300 m) high.

- Uluru is thought to be the tip of a mountain that extends many miles below the desert floor.

gorge   narrow valley between hills or mountains
rift   breaking apart, separation

Victoria Falls

One of the greatest waterfalls in the world lies where the Zambezi River drops into a deep **gorge** between Zambia and Zimbabwe in Africa. It is an amazing sight to see water spray rising over 980 feet (300 meters) in the air. The falling water makes a mighty roar as it plunges down. But the falls would not be there if the rock had not moved. The falls were formed by a deep **rift** in the rock that lies directly across the path of the Zambezi River. The rift was caused by movement of the earth's **crust** about 150 million years ago. The rock slid down, on one side of the rift, making the river fall with it.

Locals call Victoria Falls "the smoke that thunders." ▽

Trial by Water

Expanding ice

When water freezes, it turns to ice. As water freezes, it grows bigger by about 10 percent. This means that a 3.4 oz (100 ml) glass of water will freeze to give a 3.7 oz (110 ml) glass of ice. This is how water cracks, breaks, and erodes rock.

Changes happening deep underground also affect the surface of the planet. But the causes of **erosion** can be found above ground, too. Water has been shaping land for millions of years.

Slow, silent stream

About 24,000 years ago, much of the earth was covered with ice. This was called the **Ice Age.** The land was frozen. The ice was thick and very solid. But it was not still.

Slowly, over time, the **expanded** ice cut into the rock and carved **valleys** and mountains. It created some of the scenery and coastline we still see today. The coast of Norway is very rugged with a lot of small bays. These bays were carved by **glaciers.** Glaciers are ice rivers, left over from the Ice Age. They are slow and silent and they gradually **erode** rock.

◁ An **avalanche** is a dramatic example of how water in the form of snow and ice can wear away mountain rocks.

expand   make bigger
Ice Age   time when ice covered much of the world

Bird's-eye view

Marine biologists study life underwater. Marine biologist Geoff Carlier went to South America to study glacier movement. He described what he saw in his diary as he flew over some glaciers in Patagonia, southern Chile.

Glaciers can be huge. They can fill your whole field of vision with white. From the air, they look like big white highways. At the end of the glaciers are ice cliffs and **icebergs**. These are a very rich blue color. Glacier Gray is one of the biggest, and it is getting bigger all the time. The ice river flows down to a glacial lake, where there are a lot of icebergs. You can watch huge chunks of ice as big as hotels just fall off the end into the ocean.

Fragile facts

- The fastest glacier in the world is in Alaska. The Columbia Glacier can move up to 115 feet (35 meters) per day.

- The world's largest glacier is the Lambert Glacier in Antarctica. It is at least one and a half times the size of Texas.

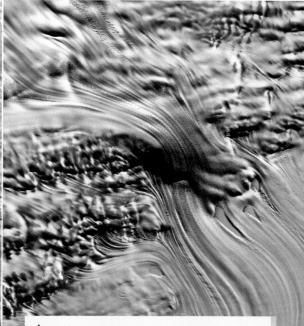

△ Pakistan has more glaciers than any other country outside the North and South Poles. The Batura Glacier is over 36 miles (58 kilometers) long.

△ The Lambert Glacier is being studied by scientists. They want to see if it can help them **predict** climate changes on the earth.

iceberg   chunk of ice that falls off a glacier into the ocean
marine biologist   scientist who studies life in the ocean

The mark of time

In the Northern Territory of Australia, Katherine Gorge has been created by a river passing through the rock over millions of years. The steep sides of the **gorge** mark the passage of the river where it has eroded the rock.

Carving canyons

Rivers flow to the oceans, leaving their dramatic mark on the landscape. The Colorado River is a winding stretch of water. It is hundreds of miles long. Over time, it has **eroded** deserts and mountains to make a passage through the land. It has even carved out the Grand **Canyon**.

The sun bakes the soil of the Grand Canyon until it is bone dry and hard. It does not rain often, but when it does the ground is too hard to **absorb** the rain. The rain pours down into the Grand Canyon, taking large rocks with it. Some of these rocks are bigger than cars. In the winter, water gets into cracks in the rocks and freezes, causing more **erosion**.

△ Katherine Gorge in Australia was created by erosion.

absorb   soak up
canyon   deep, steep valley

River ruin

Rivers all over the world erode land. Millions of people live along the world's largest rivers and depend on them for food. Rivers can be dangerous and erode structures such as buildings and bridges. When they flood they can destroy farmland and erode the soil.

About 400 million people live near the Yangtze River in China. Along the river there are forests, many different breeds of wildlife, and millions of miles of farmland. The waters of the Yangtze are used for rice **paddies** and to water wheat fields. The river flooded in 1997. Hundreds of thousands of people faced starvation because the rice and wheat crops were washed away and the land was ruined.

Water, water

The Amazon basin holds one-fifth of all the flowing water in the world. Over 1,000 rivers feed into it. If we **deforest** the area, we will lose water and land. Many animal and plant **species** would be lost forever.

The Grand Canyon follows the path of the Colorado River for ▽ over 265 miles (445 kilometers).

△ The Amazon River is the largest river in the world in terms of its volume. It runs through six South American countries including Brazil, Peru, and Ecuador.

deforest   remove forest cover from land
paddy   water-filled field for growing rice

Water, water everywhere . . .

Over 70 percent of the earth's surface is covered by water. Water has been slowly shaping the land for millions of years. It can change the landscape slowly over time or in just a matter of hours. Floods, rain, and waves all **erode** our world. **Erosion** can have serious effects on people's lives.

Disaster: Flood!

Floods are the worst kind of natural disaster because they cause the most damage. Farmland is made useless as crops are **waterlogged** and the **topsoil** is washed away. This makes it harder to plant new crops. Floods also wash away minerals in the soil that help crops to grow. Homes are destroyed and drinking water quickly gets dirty. Leaking **sewage** can **rapidly** spread disease. In poorer countries, people may have a long wait before help arrives.

River disaster

When the water level gets too high, rivers burst their banks and flood. In 1887, 900,000 people were killed when the Huang River in China burst its banks. Thousands more died from starvation and disease after the floods damaged crops.

Land near a wide river ▽ is at risk of flooding.

rapidly   with great speed
sewage   human toilet waste

Flood focus: Mozambique, 2000

The floods of 2000 were the worst to hit Mozambique, Africa for more than 150 years. A series of tropical storms caused three weeks of **severe** floods. At times, the wind reached 160 miles (260 kilometers) per hour. Over half a million people were forced to leave their homes. Roads, bridges, and farm crops were all destroyed. People who had lost everything stayed in camps, where disease spread quickly. Food was donated from other countries.

This helicopter is rescuing flood victims from a roof top in Chibuti, northern Mozambique. ▽

" From the air, the amount of water is stunning. The tops of trees and thatched huts and ruined crops are the only things you can see. "

An aid worker describing what she saw in Mozambique.

Flood figures

- The cost of flood damage in the United States is more than $3 billion a year.

- An average of 10,000 people have died each year since 1900 because of floods.

topsoil   best layer of soil for growing plants
waterlogged   soaked with water

Ebbing away?

Some of the greatest **erosion** on the planet is caused by the ocean. The ocean has the power to change coastlines, washing away rock as waves crash against it. Waves can make cliffs collapse and beaches shrink.

The South Coast Times   *January 12, 1999*

Cliff crumbles!

A huge chunk of the cliff at Beachy Head on the south coast of Britain crashed into the ocean yesterday in a massive landslide. The cliff was weakened by heavy rain and, on January 11, it crumbled. Thousands of tons of rock fell away from the cliff face. Scientists say large waves hitting the cliffs are to blame. Each time a wave hits, it sends **vibrations** up the cliff and makes the rock weaker.

The spectacular cliffs at Étretat in France were shaped over time by waves ▽ **eroding** the rock.

△ There is little left of Hallsands village today. A storm in 1917 washed most of it away.

breakwater   barrier built in oceans, seas, or lakes to protect a coast or harbor from waves

Sometimes the results of wave erosion are spectacular. In places such as Étretat, France, or the Isle of Wight in Great Britain, the waves have shaped magnificent limestone arches and pillars. Other times, the results are disastrous.

Time and tide

Over 100 years ago, many tons of **shingle** were removed from the beach of Hallsands village on the south coast of Britain. The shingle was used to build a **breakwater** in the city of Plymouth.

In the years that followed, storms continued to attack the south coast. Without the shingles there to protect the village, erosion happened quickly. With nothing to defend it against the lashing waves and howling winds, the village was swept away. Many people lost their homes and jobs.

"Feed the beach"

In some parts of the world, beaches are fed! New sand and pebbles are put on the beach to replace the ones the ocean drags away. This protects the beach and stops the waves from causing further erosion.

△ More than 1 million cubic meters of sand have now been deposited along the 3 mile (5 kilometer) shoreline of Danfuskie Island in South Carolina.

shingle pebbles
vibrations small shakes or tremors

Blowing Up a Storm

Chinese slides

In southern China in 2002, a long, hot summer meant that the earth became cracked and dry. Then **Torrential** rains came and started landslides throughout the hilly areas in the Hunan Province. Seventy people were killed.

The weather plays a part in changing the earth. Too much rain, sun, or wind can do a lot of damage to the landscape. **Weathering** is when rocks are broken down or worn away by the effects of weather. Changes in the weather can make weathering happen.

Taking a beating

Geologists study rock and how it moves and changes. They also study **erosion** and work closely with weather scientists called **meteorologists.** Between them, these scientists study how erosion and weather change the surface of the planet.

Wind, rain, and sun all erode the surface of earth. Wind picks up sand and small bits of earth and blows them away. Rain washes away **nutrients** from soil and makes it less **fertile.** Too much sunshine can kill plants, ruin crops, and make the ground too dry to grow things in it.

△ The Arches National Park in Utah is full of incredible rock formations caused by erosion.

evaporate   turn into water vapor
fertile   able to grow things

A dry spell

A **drought** happens when rainfall drops below a certain level. Where there is sunshine all the time, not many plants can grow. The sun makes water **evaporate.** This means that ponds, streams, and rivers dry up. The sun dries out the land so that it is no longer able to grow plants. Even if it does rain, the ground is too dry to soak up the water, and the **topsoil** is worn away. This means the land is useless for growing food.

El Niño

In 2002 some countries were badly affected by freak weather. *El Niño* was to blame. *El Niño* is a warming of water temperatures in the Pacific Ocean. This affects the weather around the world.

El Niño means "the Christ child" in Spanish. It is called this because it happens around Christmas every few years.

Widespread effects

In 2002 *El Niño* caused:

- droughts and flooding in South America, Australia, India, and Southeast Asia.

- heavy rain in Italy, resulting in mudslides in towns and cities.

- a record numbers of forest fires.

△ The country of Ethiopia in northeast Africa often suffers from severe drought. The average Ethiopian lives for just 43 years compared to an average of 74 years in the United States.

△ The landslide that wrecked these houses in California was caused by *El Niño.*

meteorologist   scientist who studies weather
nutrient   substance that helps things grow

Storms

Powerful winds that spin through the air are called **cyclones**. The strongest and most destructive of these winds are **hurricanes** and **tornadoes**. They also have the power to create **storm surges**. This is when the wind makes the sea rise up into giant waves that crash against the shore. These winds have the power to change the landscape in seconds.

Nightmare in paradise

In late 2002 the powerful Cyclone Zoe swept across the **remote** Solomon Islands in the Pacific Ocean. The cyclone reached speeds of over 125 miles (200 kilometers) per hour. A television cameraman who flew over the islands said, "All I saw were forests stripped bare. I could not see any homes left standing. It was total devastation."

Buildings are no match for a ▷ hurricane. With its terrific speed and strength, a hurricane will destroy everything in its path.

cyclone   powerful storm with spinning winds
hurricane   tropical storm with strong, violent winds

Savage storms

Bangladesh is a tropical country in Asia. It is large and low-lying. This means that it has a lot of land that is only just above sea level. Bangladesh often suffers from floods. The cyclone that struck the country in 1970 was the worst tropical disaster of the 20th century. More than 300,000 people died as winds of over 125 miles (200 kilometers) per hour struck the country.

The hurricane that hit Galveston, Texas, was one of the deadliest natural disasters in American history. Before the hurricane, Galveston was an ordinary town. That changed on September 8, 1900. The wind swirled around at over 140 miles (225 kilometers) per hour. There was a storm surge of 16 feet (5 meters). It cost over $20 million to repair and rebuild the town.

Counting the cost

The most expensive storm in history was Hurricane Andrew. The storm struck southern Florida in late August 1992. Andrew caused widespread damage to industry and farming. Thousands of square miles of crops were destroyed. The estimated cost was over $26 billion.

△ Hurricane Andrew was recorded traveling at speeds of 170 miles (285 kilometers) per hour.

storm surge   high waves caused by strong winds
tornado   funnel of fast, spinning wind

Wear and tear

As the wind blows, it picks up little bits of sand and earth. When this sandy wind moves across the landscape, it blows these particles against hillsides and the ground. The sandy wind wears away at mountains like sandpaper. Bits of rock are knocked off and the rock is worn away.

Crops are quickly blown down by winds like this. Because the wind also damages the soil, it is also harder to plant new crops. The central part of the United States has wide, flat fields where a lot of wheat is grown. This wheat is used for making bread, and so the whole area is called the "**breadbasket.**" When these winds whip across the land, they destroy the wheat.

Path of destruction

Every year in the United States, farmers face the threat of **tornadoes** ruining their crops. In a few seconds, a tornado can destroy a harvest.

△ This spinach field was completely wiped out by **Hurricane** Floyd in 1999.

breadbasket   area in the United States that is important for growing crops
sand dune   sand hill

Sand mountain

A **sand dune** is a mound of sand that has been left by the wind. Dunes are found in sandy areas such as coastlines and deserts. They come in many different shapes. Some are long and thin, while others are shaped like stars. The shape depends on how the wind blows the sand.

Sand dunes do not stand still. They move with the wind. If the wind is very strong, they can be carried several miles at a time. Sand dunes have ruined crops, blocked roads, and even buried houses. When the wind picks up the sand from a dune, it can **erode** rock even faster.

△ The world's longest sand dunes are along the Skeleton Coast of Namibia, in Africa.

sand sea   large area of moving sand

The Human Effect

Welsh tragedy

In 1966 in Aberfan, Wales, 144 people were killed when a **slag heap** moved after heavy rain. It slid onto a school and many children and their teachers were killed.

Humans **erode** the planet 24 hours a day, 7 days a week. Lots of things we do, from using cars to throwing away garbage, change the earth in different ways.

Food for thought

We need the earth to grow food and provide energy. Oil is pumped out of the ground to fuel our cars. Chemicals are extracted from the oil to make things ranging from building materials to medicines. We need our planet to work well, but sometimes it all goes horribly wrong.

Prince of Wales Sound, Alaska, 1991

Oil on water

Over 0.9 miles (1.4 kilometers) of coastline remain ruined by a massive oil spill two years ago. Forests, parks, and wildlife are all suffering, and thousands of birds have been poisoned. The previously beautiful coast was turned into an **oil slick** in 1989, when the *Exxon Valdez* tanker spilled enough oil to fill 125 Olympic swimming pools. Scientists fear this may be the most **environmentally** damaging oil disaster in history.

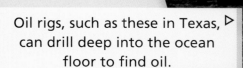

Oil rigs, such as these in Texas, ▷ can drill deep into the ocean floor to find oil.

oil slick   layer of oil floating on water
pollute   make air, water, or land dirty

Mining minerals

Coal, oil, and gold are just some of the things that we dig out of the ground. This is called mining. Most of the time, mining is safe, but when too much is taken out of the earth, it can lead to disaster.

In 1903 a small coal-mining town in Canada learned a tragic lesson. Over 70 people were killed when a landslide on Turtle Mountain devastated the town of Frank. The landslide was caused by coal-mining inside the mountain and **weathering** of the limestone on the outside of the mountain. Once the rock started to slide, there was no stopping it. Over 80 million tons of rock fell in 90 seconds. Entire houses were swallowed up.

Did you know . . . ?
Cars **pollute** the air badly. When gasoline burns, it releases poisonous gases such as carbon monoxide.

△ The air in a traffic jam is polluted by poisonous gases.

slag heap   pile of waste rock from a mining site

33

Timber!

All over the world, forests are being cut down at an alarming rate. Areas of forest are often cleared for farming. **Deforestation** is human-made destruction. The worst deforestation happens in tropical areas, such as rain forests. These forests produce a lot of the oxygen we need to breathe, and so losing them can be dangerous.

Forests are also destroyed by **pollution** from factories. Pollution happens when poison and waste enter the **environment.** The factories and cars that burn **fossil fuels,** such as coal or gas are the worst. The smoke they produce contains poisonous chemicals and gases. When these mix with water in the air, the result can be awful. Instead of normal rain falling, so that the trees in the forests can grow, something much more harmful falls out of the sky.

$$\text{rain water} + \text{harmful chemicals} = \text{acid rain}$$

Safe steps

In some tropical countries where landslides are common because of heavy rainfall, farmers "terrace" their fields. This means that they shape hillsides into steps so that crops can grow there. The plant roots help to bind the hillside together and prevent landslides.

△ Rice terraces such as these are common in China and Southeast Asia.

deforestation   when forest is removed, burned, or destroyed
fossil fuel   coal, oil, or natural gas

Acid attack

The smoke and chemicals dissolve in the rainwater and make it more acidic than normal rain. Each year, thousands of square miles of forest are affected by acid rain. It eats away at leaves and roots and eventually kills forests. When the trees are gone, the soil is soon **eroded.** Crops may not grow in these areas, and there is more danger of landslides because there are no roots to hold the earth in place.

Forest facts

- Forests cover only 25 percent of the planet's surface.
- In 2002 national park managers in the United States started to let logging and mining companies work in parks.
- 71 percent of forests in the Czech Republic are affected by acid rain.

A price to pay

We need wood for all sorts of things, from making paper to building houses. But **logging** can erode natural **habitats** for animals. It can also **pollute** rivers, and break up the forest soil structure.

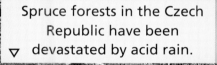

Spruce forests in the Czech Republic have been ▽ devastated by acid rain.

△ Many forests today are sustainable. This means that new trees are planted to replace those that have been cut down.

habitat   place where a plant or animal naturally lives or grows
logging   cutting down trees to sell the wood

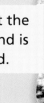

Polluted air

Making sure there is enough food for everyone is a huge business around the world. Farmland is very important in all countries. In many places, forest or grassland is cleared so that crops can be planted. This can have disastrous effects. The forests are often burned to clear them quickly and cheaply. The smoke is very dangerous to humans. It can cause **asthma** and other breathing problems.

In 2001 there were a lot of fires in Indonesia when farmers tried to clear forests. The **smog** from the fires affected 50 million people in six countries. Over 40,000 people went to the hospital because they could not breathe properly.

Did you know . . . ?

In 2003, 30 million people in Africa were at risk from **famine**. Drought was an important cause of the food shortage. Very little rain fell for two years, and so harvests failed.

△ During drought the land dries up and is easily eroded.

asthma   lung disorder that makes breathing hard
famine   serious shortage of food

Dust bowl

In the early 1900s the central and southern United States were mostly natural grassland. There were thousands of square miles of "spare" grassland, and the government wanted the land cleared to grow wheat. The wheat would then be used to make bread.

The grass was removed and wheat was planted. By 1930, however, all the soil had become dry and loose as a result of the change from grass to wheat. This part of the country is very flat and windy. The wheat did not hold the soil together and protect it from the high winds as well as the grass once had. **Drought** followed, and the soil was easily **eroded** when strong winds whipped through the region. The dust created by the soil clouds gave the area the name of the "Dust bowl."

Fragile facts

- The type of grass that was cleared away in the Midwest before the 1930s is now planted to stop **sand dunes** from moving. It is called esparto.

- The Aral Sea in Asia is shrinking. Much of its water was taken away for farming, and the sea has started to dry up.

Giant dust storms in the dry Midwest have been known to ▽ block out the Sun for several days.

△ The Aral Sea was once the fourth largest inland sea in the world. Now it is drying up.

smog   fog-like haze caused by smoke or pollution

Off the beaten track?

Everyone loves to go on vacation. But when a lot of people want to do the same thing, it can cause problems for the **environment**. The movement of all these people on the earth's surface **erodes** the rock and soil over time.

Kate and Ben Smee traveled to see Yellowstone National Park, which is mostly in Wyoming. They were hoping to find some peace and quiet in the natural **wilderness**. They were **dismayed** to find themselves in the middle of an enormous traffic jam. "It was incredible," Kate said. "End to end cars throughout the park."

Sarah Morris was very excited as she packed her backpack to go on a safari in Tanzania. But it was not exactly the wild Africa she had been hoping for. "There were 30 large jeeps full of tourists parked around a tiny hippo pool. It was like being in a traffic jam," she said.

Spoiled beauty

Many people traveling means more **pollution**. There will be fumes from cars, buses, and airplanes. There will also be more litter. This will affect beautiful places where people travel.

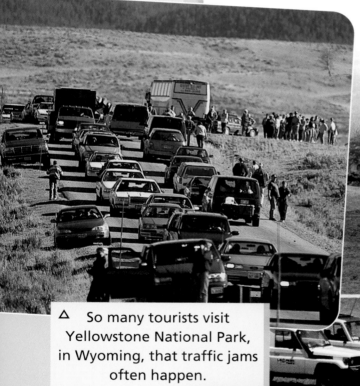

△ So many tourists visit Yellowstone National Park, in Wyoming, that traffic jams often happen.

dismayed   extremely disappointed
ecosystem   relationship between animals and their environment

A great barrier

Imagine a chain of millions and millions of multicolored animals and plants living in a clear blue sea. Each tiny piece of that living chain is an important part of one of the biggest, most important, and **fragile ecosystems** on Earth: the Great Barrier Reef.

The Great Barrier Reef lies off the coast of Australia. It is thousands of miles long. Every year thousands of visitors come to dive and snorkel. Amelia Brock went diving in this natural wonder. "It was absolutely amazing. All the fish and coral were so brightly colored and there were so many of them! But you could see damaged and dead coral where diving equipment had been dropped onto the reef. There were also lots of boats **moored** near the reef with their engine fumes and oil spilling out."

Crowds flock to photograph animals in the Ngorungora Conservation Area in Tanzania, East Africa. They could be destroying the **habitat** of the very animals they come to see. ▽

△ The Great Barrier Reef attracts thousands of divers every year.

moored   tied up
monitor   check

Erosion in the Future

Ice caps

- The North and South Poles are massive areas of ice.

- They are home to many plants and animals, such as penguins and polar bears.

- If the earth gets hotter, the ice will melt and sea levels will rise, causing flooding.

The **greenhouse effect** is actually a natural **process** that controls the balance of heat inside the earth's **atmosphere**. The gases in our atmosphere trap some of the Sun's heat as it is reflected back to space. This makes the earth about 90 °F (30 °C) hotter than it would be otherwise. So natural greenhouse gases are important for all living things. But when humans release carbon dioxide and water vapor into the atmosphere, these gases add to the natural greenhouse effect, heating up the planet more than usual. This is known as **global warming.** Scientists have predicted that the temperature everywhere on the earth will rise by several degrees over the next 100 years.

Global warming could melt huge areas of the planet's ice caps. This would cause ▽ flooding around the world.

△ The **habitats** of Arctic and Antarctic animals are under threat.

atmosphere   layer of gases surrounding the earth and other planets
global warming   rise in the earth's temperature over time

Hole in the ozone layer

A layer of ozone gas surrounds the earth and filters out some of the harmful ultraviolet (UV) light rays from the Sun. These UV rays cause sunburn and skin cancer. Gases called chlorofluorocarbons (CFCs), used in refrigeration, air-conditioning, cleaning solvents, packing materials, and aerosol sprays, damage the **ozone layer** and make it thinner. UV rays can pass through gaps in the ozone layer, damaging living things. The thinning of the ozone layer also adds to global warming. The use of CFCs in aerosols has now been banned in many countries. But other chemicals, such as nitrogen oxides from fertilizers, may also attack the ozone layer.

The forecast

Global warming may cause dramatic changes in the weather. Summers might become extremely hot and cause deserts and **droughts.** Winters might be **severely** cold. Sea levels would rise as the polar caps melt, causing flooding in low-lying countries. Spring rains might cause rivers to have burst their banks, ruining farmland. Nobody can be sure exactly what global warming will bring, but the changes in the weather may speed up the **erosion** of the planet's surface.

Warming planet

- Global temperatures have risen a significant amount over the last 100 years.

- Some scientists think that because of global warming, parts of the United States could be underwater by 2050.

greenhouse effect   trapping of heat by water vapor, carbon dioxide, and other gases

Knowledge is the key

Around the world, there are efforts to reduce erosion and pollution caused by humans and natural sources. The more we know, the more we can do to prevent further damage. We can all do our part.

A cycle of renewal

Erosion does not always destroy the planet. Sometimes nature recycles materials over thousands of years. The rock cycle is like this. Mountains are worn away and the small pieces that are **eroded** become soil. Soil is blown or washed away to become **compressed** as new rock on the ocean floor. In other places, volcanic **eruptions** will create new mountains. So the land does renew itself, but it takes a very, very long time.

Making a difference

Many groups and organizations work hard to make the earth safer and cleaner. Greenpeace and Friends of the Earth are two international organizations that talk to governments and people about environmental **issues.** Being "green" means you are helping the planet by recycling things or trying to stop **pollution.**

△ Groins are built out from beaches to trap sand and **shingle.**

Many teams of **volunteers** ▷ work to repair the effects of erosion in their spare time.

compress   squeeze together
issue   important subject for discussion

Erosion can be controlled through sensible farming and **logging,** and by being more careful with our waste products. For many people, it is a choice about they way they live. We can all make a very quick difference if we do not produce so much garbage ourselves. Things such as cans and bottles can be recycled so they do not clog up garbage dumps. Could all fast-food wrappers and packages be avoided?

The future

Every single day, the earth crumbles a little bit more. Some of this erosion is natural. Some of it is not. Land, water, wind, and humans all play their part in the changing face of our planet. Some things can be used again. Some things do not have a second chance. Think about it.

After all, there is only one Earth.

Health risk

Mexico City is the most polluted major city on Earth. The air is so bad, there is a **permanent** haze, or **smog,** over the city. Millions of people who live there have breathing problems.

Some residents of Mexico City wear masks to protect themselves from harmful smog. ▽

permanent always there
volunteer person who is working for free

43

Find Out More

Organizations

U.S. Geological Survey

The national site for landslide information in the United States, including news on the most recent landslides.

landslides.usgs.gov

Center for Integration of Natural Disaster Information

The CINDI website contains a lot of information on landslides, floods, hurricanes, droughts, and other natural disasters and storms.

cindi.usgs.gov

Books

Spilsbury, L., and R. Spilsbury. *Awesome Forces of Nature: Crushing Avalanches*. Chicago: Heinemann Library, 2003.

Hunter, Rebecca. *Discovering Geography: Weather*. Chicago: Raintree, 2003.

Morris, Neil. *Landscapes and People: Earth's Changing Mountains*. Chicago: Raintree, 2003.

Redmond, Jim, and Ronda Redmond. *Nature on the Rampage: Landslides*. Chicago: Raintree, 2003.

World Wide Web

If you want to find out more about landslides and **erosion,** you can search the Internet using keywords such as these:

- landslide + news + [date you are interested in]
- "acid rain" + landslide
- **deforestation** + erosion
- effects + **"global warming"**
- **plate tectonics**

You can also find your own keywords by using headings or words from this book. Use the search tips on page 45 to help you find the most useful websites.

Search tips

There are billions of pages on the Internet, so it can be difficult to find exactly what you want to find. For example, if you just type in "water" in a search engine such as Google, you will get a list of 85 million web pages! These search skills will help you find useful websites more quickly:

- Know exactly what you want to find out about first.
- Use simple keywords instead of whole sentences.
- Use two to six keywords in a search, putting the most important words first.
- Be precise—only use names of people, places, or things.
- If you want to find words that go together, put quote marks around them—for example, "**sand dune**" or "acid rain."
- Use the advanced section of your search engine.
- Use the + sign to add certain words.

Where to search

Search engine

A search engine looks through the entire web and lists all the sites that match the words in the search box. They can give thousands of links, but the best matches are at the top of the list, on the first page. Try **google.com**.

Search directory

A search directory is more like a library of websites that have been sorted by a person instead of a computer. You can search by keyword or subject and browse through the different sites in the same way you would look through books on a library shelf. A good example is **yahooligans.com**.

Glossary

absorb   soak up

asthma   lung disorder that makes breathing hard

atmosphere   layer of gases surrounding Earth and other planets

avalanche   mass of snow, ice, rocks, or mud falling quickly down a mountain

breadbasket   area in the United States that is important for growing crops

breakwater   barrier built in the sea to protect a coast or harbor from waves

buckle   twist or bend out of shape

canyon   deep, steep valley

compress   squeeze together

continent   one of the earth's seven large land masses

core   ultrahot center of the earth

crust   earth's outer layer of rock

cyclone   powerful storm with spinning winds

deforest   to remove forest cover from land

deforestation   process of removing, burning, or destroying

dismayed   extremely disappointed

drought   severe lack of rainfall over time, causing crops to die

ecosystem   relationship between animals and their environment

environment   natural world around us

environmental   having to do with the environment

epicenter   point at which an earthquake reaches the earth's surface

erode   slowly wear away

erosion   wearing away of the earth's surface

eruption   explosion of a volcano

estimate   make an educated guess

evaporate   turn water into water vapor

expand   make bigger

extinct   exists no more

famine   serious shortage of food that leads many to starvation

fertile   able to grow things

focus   source of an earthquake deep underground

fossil fuel   coal, oil, or natural gas

fragile   delicate

geologist   scientist who studies rocks

glacier   slow-moving river of ice

global warming   rise in the earth's temperature over time

gorge   narrow valley between hills or mountains

greenhouse effect   trapping of heat by water vapor, carbon dioxide and other gases

habitat   place where a plant or animal naturally lives or grows

hurricane   tropical storm with strong, violent winds

Ice Age   time when ice covered much of the world

iceberg   chunk of ice that falls off a glacier into the sea

issue   important subject for discussion

logging   cutting down trees to sell the wood

magma extremely hot melted rock and gas underground

mantle hot gases and metals that surround the earth's core

marine biologist scientist who studies life in the oceans

meteorologist scientist who studies weather

molten melted

monitor to watch closely

moored tied up

nutrient substance that helps things grow

oil slick layer of oil floating on water

ozone layer layer of gas in the upper atmosphere that protects the earth from the Sun's harmful ultraviolet (UV) rays

paddy water-filled field for growing rice

permanent always there

plate tectonics movement of the earth's plates

pollute make air, water, or land dirty

pollution harmful things in air, in water, or on land

precious valuable, important

predict informed guess that something will happen in the future

process series of steps

rapidly with great speed

remote long distance away

rift breaking apart, separation

sand dune hill made of drifting sand

sand sea large area of moving sand

severe very bad or serious

sewage human toilet waste

shingle large pebbles on the shores of a body of water

shockwaves forces that are created by an earthquake deep underground

slag heap pile of waste rock from a mining site

smog fog-like haze caused by smoke or pollution

species types of plant or animal

storm surge high waves caused by strong winds

topsoil top layer of soil. It is the best for growing plants

tornado funnel of fast, spinning wind

torrential strong, fast-moving

trigger cause something

tsunami huge ocean wave caused by an earthquake, landslide, or volcanic eruption

valley low area of land between hills or mountains

vent hole in the earth's crust

vibrations small shakes or tremors

volunteer person who is working for free

waterlogged soaked with water

weathering breakdown of rocks by exposure to weather

wilderness undisturbed or wild natural area

Index